Tears to Strength
A Daughter's Grief

Sharon Fernandes

BookLeaf
Publishing

India | USA | UK

Tears to Strength : A Daughter's Grief ©
2024 Sharon Fernandes

All rights reserved.

No part of this publication may be
reproduced, stored in a retrieval system, or
transmitted, in any form or by any means,
electronic, mechanical, photocopying,
recording or otherwise, without the prior
written permission of the presenters.

Sharon Fernandes asserts the moral right to
be identified as the author of this work.

Presentation by *BookLeaf Publishing*

Web: www.bookleafpub.com

E-mail: info@bookleafpub.com

ISBN: 9789363308275

First edition 2024

To my dearest Paa,

Your memory is the light that guides me through the darkest times. This book is dedicated to you for teaching me the true meaning of strength, resilience and unconditional love. Though you are no longer by my side, your presence is felt every moment, and your legacy lives on in my heart. This journey is a testament to your profound impact on my life.

With all my love,

Sharon Fernandes.

ACKNOWLEDGEMENTS

Writing this book has been an incredibly personal and transformative journey.

First and foremost, I would like to thank God for bestowing upon me the talent and passion for writing. His divine inspiration has fuelled my creativity and provided me with the words to express my thoughts and emotions.

I would also want to thank my beloved father. Although you are no longer physically here, your love, wisdom and guidance have continued to inspire me every day. This book is a testament to the profound impact you have had on my life, and I hope it honours your memory in a way that reflects the depth of my gratitude and love.

To my family and friends, who have been my rock and shared in this grief and healing, your presence in my life is a constant source of strength, comfort and encouragement.

To my editor and publishing team, thank you for believing in this project and for helping me to shape my words into a book that I am proud to share with the world. Your expertise, dedication and guidance have been instrumental in bringing this book to life.

Finally, to my readers, thank you for taking the time to engage with my poems. It is my hope that this book provides comfort, hope and a sense of connection to those who are navigating their own journeys of loss and healing. Your support and feedback are deeply appreciated, and I am grateful for the opportunity to share this journey with you.

With deepest gratitude,
Sharon Fernandes.

PREFACE

Losing a father is a profound and life-altering experience. The journey from the depths of grief to the heights of strength is one that many must undertake, but it is a path often walked alone. This book is born out of my personal journey through this heart-wrenching transformation after the loss of my beloved father.

In the wake of my dad's passing, I found myself engulfed in a sea of tears, struggling to navigate a world that seemed to have lost its anchor. The void left by his absence was overwhelming, and the grief threatened to consume me. It was during these darkest moments that I began to seek out the fragments of strength he had instilled in me throughout my life.

This book is not just about my own healing; it is a ray of hope for anyone who has lost a loved one. It is a reminder that grief is a universal experience. It is the raw, unfiltered expression of love in its purest form. Grief is more than just a response to death. This book is not just a collection of poems but a journey for those navigating through the turbulent waters of loss.

As we embark on this journey together, let us honour the memory of those we've lost, not by letting their absence consume us, but by cherishing the moments we shared and the love that bound us together. For in the darkness of loss, we discover the light of love that will guide us through the darkest of nights.

To anyone who is grieving, I offer my heartfelt empathy and understanding. Know you are not alone in this; we grieve together and strengthen together. May these pages provide comfort and inspiration, and may you find your own path from tears to strength.

With love and remembrance,
Sharon Fernandes.

Table of Contents

WATCHING HIM FADE AWAY

(Just before he went to a better place)

Nothing is more painful than
watching your loved one shrink in front of you.
Nothing is more depressing than
watching his smile fade.

Helplessness covers you,
You realise you are weak.
You stand, holding his feet as he looks at you,
Seeming to understand without words.

Tears you swallow,
To show him you're strong,
Holding his hand and assuring,
All the wrongs will soon be gone.

Praying every second
For him to come back home,
For his smile to return,
For the suffering to leave him alone.

With a burden in my heart,
I melt away in shame,
As I have nothing to offer
To someone who gave his all to me.

I will wait for you with hope in my heart,
Trusting in the ultimate healer.
Forever, you hold the best place in my heart—
Forever, you are my hero.

SILENT FAREWELL

The song has lost its tune now,
You sing at home no more,
I wonder why you went away—
So far, it's still unknown.

It hurts to see your pictures,
So happy and so bold.
I think of how you slept, Paa,
So quiet and so cold.

I can't imagine what you thought last;
Why didn't you call for me?
I wonder if you ever knew
How hurtful this farewell would be.

I see a dead end in front of me;
I see it's dark and cold.
I don't know who will shelter me now—
I pray; my hands now fold.

Your silent farewell leaves me broken.
Silent tears flow down my face.
Silently, my life seems shattered,
Silently, as you fade away.

DROWNING IN GRIEF

*I call you from my phone, hoping you will answer
someday,
Imagine you walking into the house, calling my
name.
I wish I could make coffee for you again–
My dearest Paa, I miss you more than words can
explain.*

*I dream, and in my dreams, I see you laughing;
I wake up and find you gone.
Tears roll down my face, and I am weeping:
Why, Paa, did you go so far?*

*Your voice I hear and will remember always,
Your words weigh more than ever now.
I see the disappearance of all my pathways;
Without you, where do I go, and how?*

In my heart, you live forever,
Someone who can never leave.
I'm lost in this world all alone–
Please help me move out of this zone.

STRUGGLE TO SAY GOODBYE

When the heart struggles,
Your tears begin to flow.
You look up to the heavens,
As you don't find answers anymore.

When your heart struggles,
Each breath you take is slow.
Struggling through the silence,
The way forward seems unknown.

When the heart struggles,
You wish your pain could fly.
You struggle to live in this endless sorrow,
A little strength you wish you could borrow.

As days blend into night,
I hold onto memories, vivid and bright.
I struggle to find hope in tomorrow,
Yearning for peace and strength to follow.

RAW FEELINGS OF GRIEF

My heart is broken,
It's aching deep inside.
I am on my knees,
No help left to stand.

Since you are not around,
I don't know where to look.
There are questions overflowing,
And the grief within me is ruling.

The pain travels from my eyes;
It pierces my heart.
I scream out loud
Until I can't breathe anymore.

I sit on the floor,
And I wonder where you are.
Can you see the tears rolling down my face?
Can you feel my heart burning?

I know you are in a better place,
But did you think of me?
My heart is tearing
Now that you are not with me.

MY FOUNDATION

My foundation of life is shaken,
My heart sinks with grief.
The achievements I have made are meaningless,
As I stand here feeling weak.

My life has come to a standstill,
I can't believe my eyes.
You said you would come home to me,
But how could you say 'Goodbye'?

You always told me this day would come;
No one can prepare for this.
It's not right for you to leave me alone,
Or leave me without a hint.

You taught me everything about life,
But today you taught me the real definition of
'Separation' and 'Death'.
Indeed, they are enemies,
I don't think I can heal myself.

I hope to see you as an angel.
I hope I can hug you and say
How much I miss you
Every single day.

IN THE SHADOW OF LOSS

*It's raining, Paa. I remember your prayers for
'rain'.
The weather is chilly and calm.
Don't you want to feel it again?*

*The silence is killing.
I wish you could know.
I am heartbroken.
Don't leave me alone.*

*The world is sailing on the sea,
It's stormy and dark.
You would have held onto me—
You were my ark.*

I remember you in the morning.
I miss you at noon.
I sit on your bed in the evening.
In my dreams, I will see you soon.

You helped me get stronger, Paa.
I remind myself I am a strong man's daughter.
I will move slowly,
But please show me the path I need to go.

THROUGH THE VOID

The world feels emptier today.
My life feels cold.
The roads seem longer today.
I don't have anyone to hold.

I miss you, Paa,
More than words can express.
My anchor in times of challenge,
My joy, and now my pain.
I'm haunted by a void;
I'm going insane.

In this void,
I navigate through endless nights,
Reaching out for the dawn,
A distant light.

In this void,
There is a fragile hope
That I'll find grace and strength to cope.

LOST IN MOURNING

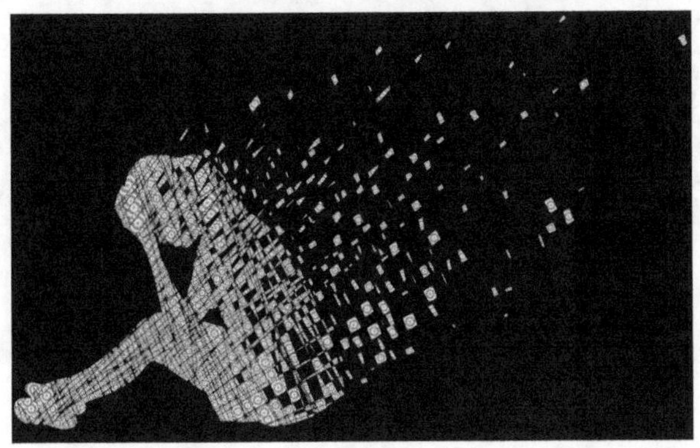

The inner me screams with sorrow,
But my face stays calm.
The inner me cries in pain,
But I say I'm alright.

Losing a father is like losing a part of your life.
You live because you have to.
It takes away the joy and peace;
It takes away the strength you have in yourself.

Every smile seems fake.
Every achievement seems just for its own sake.
I don't know what to make of this.
I guess the healing is learning 'to get stronger'.
I wish, Paa, you lived longer.

WHISPERS OF THE PAST

The days keep running by;
The nights move on.
The memories of your stay—
They linger forever on.

The foundation of your love
It's rooted deep in my heart.
Nothing can take its place, Paa,
So, I stay strong in my heart.

You always heard my silent screams, Paa,
When I shouted in pain.
You read my disturbed mind, Paa,
You were with me every day.

My pillar and my comfort, Paa,
You will always be.
I know you are right here, Paa;
Forever close to me.

LOVE BEYOND THE VEIL

Your voice is like a whisper on the breeze;
Your smile is a warmth that never leaves.
In every moment, big or small,
I feel your love – I hear your call.

Though time has taken you away,
In my heart, you'll always stay–
As a living light that guides me through.
To thoughts of you, I'm always glued.

Though absent from my sight and touch,
You're in my life; you mean so much.
In memories, you are not lost;
You live on at every heartbeat's cost.

In each warm hug, each gentle touch,
Your presence feels so close, so much.
In moments bright and as shadows cast,
You're with me now and will always last.

TIMELESS BOND

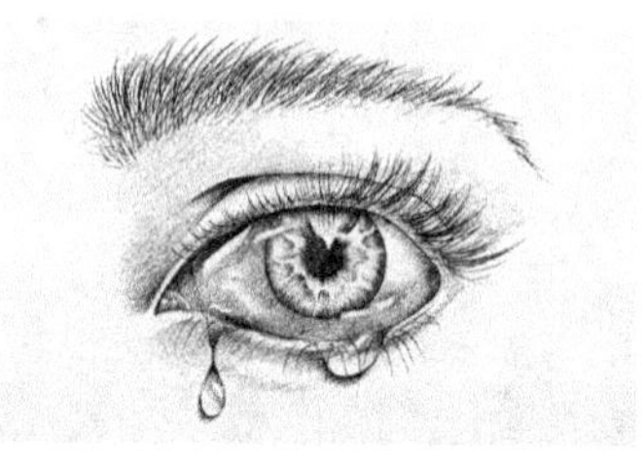

As I hear someone call 'Paa',
Your face appears in my mind.
A tear drops down,
And my eyes close
As your memories splash before me.

My laughter, my joy, my strength seem gone
As you silently slipped away.
Where do I go to hear your voice again?
Where do I stand to see your smile?

I look within me
And find you there.
You are my heartbeat;
You are the power within.

I try to strengthen my legs
To stand and push myself to move ahead.
You are my determination, Paa;
You live forever within me.

THE WEIGHT OF ABSENCE

Your chair sits empty, a hollow space,
Where laughter danced and filled the place.
A daily ritual, now turned to dust,
In echoes of memories, I find my trust.

The walls still whisper of stories shared,
Moments of triumph when you truly cared.
Your voice, a melody that once rang clear,
Now lingers softly, a haunting presence near.

I remember the warmth of your steady hand,
Guiding me gently, helping me stand.
Through life's wild storms, you taught me to fight,
To find my strength, to seek the light.

Yet now, in the silence, I feel the weight
Of unspoken words and love's cruel fate.
Grief is a journey, a winding road,
With peaks of sorrow and valleys of load.

But in this heaviness, I start to see
The lessons you left, the gift to be free.
No longer can I waste my heart on the small,
For life's too precious, and I stand tall.

Each tear I shed becomes a seed,
Growing resilience, my spirit freed.
From the ashes of loss, a fire ignites,
In the shadows of grief, my heart now fights.

I gather the moments that shaped who I am,
The love that remains, the strength in my hand.
Your absence is heavy, yet I rise anew;
In every heartbeat, I feel you too.

So here I stand, in the light of your grace,
With courage unyielding, I embrace my place.
Your chair may be empty, but your love's still alive;
In the depths of my heart, I learn to thrive.

WHISPERS OF YOUR LIGHT

In the quiet of my mind, your smiling face appears,
A light of warmth, dissolving all my fears.
Your charm was a gift, a light in every room,
A laughter like sunshine, chasing away the gloom.

I see you standing tall, sharing wisdom and grace,
Preaching love and kindness, a smile on your face.
Moments spent together, sipping tea with delight,
Conversations lingered, weaving joy through the
night.

Your laughter, a melody that echoes in my heart,
In the fabric of memories, you play the finest part.
With every shared story, I find pieces of you,
In the warmth of your memories, your love shines
through.

Though the sorrow of losing you pulls me down
low,

*In the richness of your memory, your essence will
grow.
For in every smile I share, in every kind deed,
I'll carry your charm with me, in thought, word
and deed.*

*So, here's to the moments, the laughter, the tea,
To the love that you gave, that forever will be.
Though I miss you deeply, I'll hold your light near,
In the smile on my face, I'll remember you here.*

MORNING MELODIES

Each morning dawned with a gentle tune,
As sunlight spilled across the room.
Your voice, Paa, was a sweet embrace,
A melody that filled our space.

I'd wake to songs, soft and bright,
Carried on the wings of light.
You sang of love, of joy, of grace,
Setting the tone for each day to face.

Your laughter mingled with every note,
In those moments, my heart would float.
With each refrain, worries would fade,
A morning ritual that joyfully played.

Though the days have changed and you are gone,
Your songs still echo, a cherished dawn.
In my heart, your melodies stay,
A love-filled tune that guides my way.

A LEGACY IN STYLE

In college halls, there walked a man,
With style and grace, the best in the land.
Paa, you carried yourself with such flair,
Every outfit, a statement beyond compare.

With tailored suits and shirts pressed right,
You turned every head, a true delight.
From polished shoes to a confident stance,
You taught the world the art of elegance.

Your laughter echoed, a charming sound,
As you made every moment feel profound.
Not just in clothes, but in the love you'd share,
You dressed my heart with thoughtful care.

In every gathering, you'd shine like a star,
A path of elegance, no matter how far.
Your style was more than just fabric and thread;
It was the warmth of your spirit, the love you
spread.

Now as I recall those days gone by,
I see your legacy, and I can't help but sigh.
For in your best-dressed moments, I see
A father's love, forever stylishly free.

DANCING THROUGH MEMORIES

As the stars begin to twinkle and glow,
I sit in the stillness, missing you so.
The echoes of music fill the night air,
With memories of moments we used to share.

We'd sing our hearts out, ABBA on repeat,
'Take a Chance on Me', tapping our feet.
Your smile lit the room, your joy so sincere—
In those simple times, you felt so near.

And in the hush, your voice would rise;
With Don Moen's songs, we'd touch the skies.
'Thank You, Lord', you'd sing with such grace,
Faith and love shining bright on your face.

Though days feel heavy and nights stretch long,
In every note played, I hear our song.
I'll keep singing our favourites, holding them tight,
For in every chorus, you're still my light.

THE GUIDING VOICE

I remember the night before my first seminar;
Nerves were dancing; everything felt so bizarre.
But you sat with me, calm and wise–
Every word you spoke opened my eyes.

'Just be yourself; you've got this, magalae',
Your voice, a melody, kept all doubts away.
You helped me outline my thoughts with care,
Turning chaos to clarity – a beautiful pair.

With each practice run, you cheered me on;
Your belief in me felt like a warm dawn.
'Imagine them smiling; they're here to learn'–
You lit a spark, a steady, deep burn.

As the day approached, my heart raced so fast,
But you stood beside me, shadows were cast.
'Remember our songs; let the joy take flight;
You carry my love; you'll shine so bright'.

Now I stand tall, my voice strong and clear;
With every success, I feel you near.
Thank you for being my anchor, my guide–
In the journey of life, I walk with pride.

IN EVERY QUIET MOMENT

I miss you, Paa, in the softest ways,
In the echoes that linger through each day.
When morning light filters gently through,
I am reminded of everything you used to do.

You sat with me, patient and kind,
Guiding each word, expanding my mind.
With every page turned, your voice a guide—
Reading became a shared stride.

After a bath, when droplets clung,
Your hands worked gently; songs were sung.
You dried my hair with tender care;
In those moments, love was everywhere.

I remember you by the college gate—
A familiar face, there to wait.
Dropping me off with a smile so bright,
Picking me up as day turned to night.

Now, those drives are memories, gold,
Stories treasured, never growing old.
A presence felt in each little thing,
In autumn's breeze, in the warmth of spring.

Though you're gone, I still find you here,
In laughter, in whispers, in every tear.
Your love, so deep, never parts;
It lives on, etched within my heart.

In every quiet moment, you remain—
A father's love, endless, without refrain.

TENDER TOUCHES

I miss those moments, so simple, so true–
Scratching your back, just me and you.
My hands in your hair, a gentle caress;
In those quiet times, I found my rest.

Holding your legs, a bond felt clear;
With every touch, I felt you near.
The warmth of your presence, a comforting balm–
In the embrace of your love, my heart stayed calm.

You taught me that comfort is more than a touch;
It's the care and kindness that mean so much.
In those shared moments, I felt so alive–
A connection so deep, it helped me thrive.

Now as I sit with these memories so dear,
I cherish each gesture, though you're not here.
For in every scratch, every soothing embrace,
I hold onto the love that time can't erase.

So, I'll carry your spirit in all that I do;
In the tender touches, I'll always find you.
For the bond that we shared will never depart–
You live on forever within my heart.

LATE NIGHT MEMORIES

In the still of the night, when the world's in dream,
I think of the moments, the memories that gleam.
Our binge-watch marathons till the crack of dawn,
With laughter and stories, all worries withdrawn.

We'd sink into cushions, lost in the screen's glow,
Crime flicks light up each twist and flow.
Sharing your wild thoughts on each shocking turn–
In those late-night hours, so much left to learn.

And how we'd sing out, our voices a blend,
Echoing softly, with you as my friend.
Each song we'd create, a bond we'd ignite–
In those treasured times, everything felt right.

Now here in the silence, I miss your bright spark,
The thrill of our talks, our adventures till dark.
The chase in movies, the songs that we'd share–
In this quiet, your absence hangs heavy in the air.

So, here's to the nights and the shows we adored,
To the love and the laughter, the joy we explored.
Though series may end and those movies may fade,
In my heart, those moments will never degrade.

CLASSROOM OF MEMORIES

In the quiet halls where echoes roam,
A place of learning, a second home.
There you stood, poised and wise,
With a familiar light in your eyes.

'Attendance', you'd call, voice so clear,
And I'd answer, trying not to cheer.
The world saw a professor, composed and grand,
But I saw my father, a steady hand.

Each lesson you taught held more than facts;
It carried warmth in all its acts.
Your words wove stories, sharp and true,
Bringing life to things I never knew.

I'd watch as students leaned in,
Unaware of where I'd been.
They didn't know the man who read,
Who tucked me in, who kissed my head.

Yet there you were, with that same care,
In every lecture, in each knowing stare.
Pride would swell, my heart would race,
Hearing you speak, holding your place.

Though you're gone, your lessons stay,
Guiding me through each passing day.
Professor, father, mentor, friend–
Your love, my compass, without end.

MORE THAN A TEACHER

Paa, you were more than a teacher to all,
A man of wisdom, standing tall.
When you walked in, voices would still;
Eyes followed you, with a silent thrill.

You weren't just my father, but a guide,
A beacon of warmth, with arms open wide.
Students would gather, seeking your care,
Asking you softly for a moment of prayer.

And you'd smile in that gentle way–
Hands clasped, with comforting words to say.
A blessing spoken, calm and bright,
Turning their worries into light.

I'd watch, my heart swelling with pride,
Seeing the faith others held inside.
You were the one who comforted me at night,
And wiped my tears until all felt right.

You were more than titles or degrees;
A quiet strength beneath the trees,
A steadfast force, my dearest friend,
A father whose love would never end.

Though time has taken you from here,
Your legacy remains, ever near—
In every story, every prayer,
In echoes of footsteps on the stair.

They looked up to you, and so did I,
With every breath, every sigh.
Proud to be yours, proud to see,
The man who shaped so much of me.

COFFEE WITH MEMORIES

I miss the mornings, soft and slow,
When dawn's first light began to glow.
You'd make the coffee, rich and warm—
A simple act, a cherished norm.

We'd sit together, cups in hand,
Talking about life, trying to understand.
Your voice, a blend of wisdom and grace,
Filled that quiet, sacred space.

We'd speak of dreams, both big and small,
Of victories won, and times we'd fall.
You shared your stories, lessons learned,
And from those moments, my heart turned.

Talks of God, of faith's embrace,
Of finding light in the darkest place.
You spoke of love, of loss and the fight,
To seek what's true, to hold on tight.

Now the mornings feel a little less,
Without your voice, without your presence.
The coffee brews, the sun still climbs,
But silence stretches through those times.

Yet, in every sip, in every thought,
I hear your laughter, lessons you taught.
In the stillness, your echoes remain,
Guiding me through joy and pain.

So, though I miss those morning talks,
The wisdom in my heart still walks.
Carrying you in all I do–
A father's love, constant and true.

THE WELL OF WISDOM

Paa, you were more than just a name,
A pillar strong, an eternal flame.
In every word, in every deed,
A life of wisdom, a path to lead.

Your knowledge was as deep as the sea,
Endless, vast and guiding me.
Lessons on life, both harsh and kind,
Taught me courage and strength of mind.

I'd watch you, captivated, in quiet awe—
Your clarity in every answer, every law.
The way you'd share, so calm, so clear,
Made every doubt disappear.

Stories of old and tales of truth,
Roots of wisdom from your youth.
You'd teach of patience, faith and light,
Of battles fought, wrongs made right.

With each question, you'd never rush,
A thoughtful pause, a gentle hush.
You'd impart the knowledge you bore—
A father, a teacher and so much more.

Now, in moments when I'm lost,
When life demands its heavy cost,
I find your words, a steady guide,
An echo strong I hold inside.

Your wisdom, Paa, a gift so rare,
A beacon bright, beyond compare.
Though you're gone, your voice remains,
In every choice, in all my gains.

And as I walk through this vast span,
I see you, wise and kind, my guiding man.
Your legacy, a timeless blend—
A father's knowledge, without end.

TO MY SELFLESS FATHER

Paa, if words could capture your soul,
They'd tell of a heart, generous and whole.
A life lived for others, never for show,
A quiet grace that seemed to glow.

You gave without question, without need,
Every action, a thoughtful deed.
Whether in kindness or in the care you shared,
You showed what it meant to truly be there.

I watched you face life's ceaseless demands,
With an open heart and outstretched hands.
Sacrifices made without a sigh,
A selfless love that reached the sky.

You were calm in every storm,
A shelter safe, a place so warm.
Your gracious spirit, so bright,
Guiding us all, day and night.

No task too small, no burden too great,
You gave your all, an unwavering state.
In your presence, I always knew,
A love so deep, steady and true.

Now, as I walk this path alone,
I carry your lessons, fully grown.
To give, to love, to lift and mend,
To be the friend on whom others depend.

Thank you, Paa, for teaching me,
What selfless, gracious love could be.
Your generous heart still beats in mine,
A legacy – timeless, pure and divine.

And though you're gone, your spirit stays,
In all my steps, in all my days.
I strive to be the daughter you'd see,
Worthy of your boundless legacy.

THE LIFTER OF BURDENS

Paa, you were the peace within the chaos,
A haven so safe, steady and warm.
With just a smile or a knowing look,
You'd lift the weight that life once took.

In moments when worry clouded my day,
You'd find the words to chase it away.
A joke, a story, a simple cheer,
And suddenly, everything felt clear.

Your laughter, rich and full of light,
Turned dark days into something bright.
The world seemed gentler when you were near,
A voice of reason, love and cheer.

When stress built up, too heavy to bear,
You'd remind me of hope and dare.
'Let it go; it will be fine', you'd say,
With a wisdom so divine, lighting the way.

With every hug and calming tone,
You made me feel I wasn't alone.
You'd chase the shadows far away,
Making room for a brighter day.

Now, in moments when life weighs down,
I close my eyes, and there's that sound–
Your voice reminds me to breathe,
To let my worries slowly leave.

Though you're gone, your strength remains,
A balm for heartache, for life's strains.
I carry your gift, so rare and true,
The courage to find peace, thanks to you.

Thank you, Paa, for every sigh,
For teaching me to let stress fly.
Your love, a light that never departs,
Forever easing and lifting hearts.

A FATHER'S FAITH

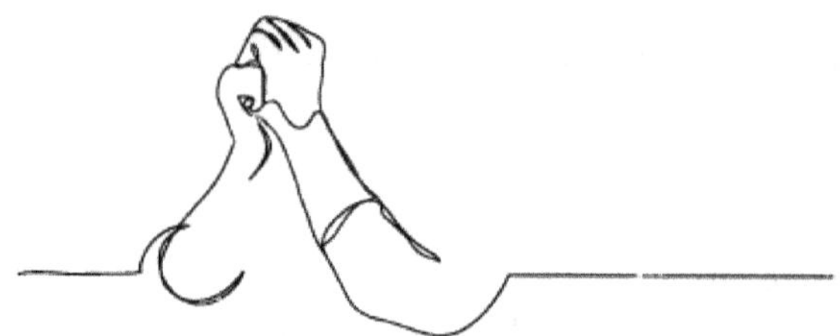

Paa, you were a preacher, wise and strong,
With a voice that echoed true and long.
You spoke of God's love, of grace so pure,
A guiding presence, steadfast and sure.

In every sermon, your passion shone,
Teaching me lessons that I've now grown.
You shared the ways of kindness and peace,
A path to follow, where worries cease.

Your words were a melody, soothing and clear;
In the depths of my heart, I hold them dear.
You taught me to walk in goodness each day,
To find the light, and choose the way.

With every prayer, you'd lift my goal,
Showing me how to make myself whole.
In your embrace, I felt your light,

A reflection of love, eternally bright.

You spoke of compassion, of lending a hand,
Of understanding and love, a life so grand.
Your faith was a beacon, a guiding star,
Leading me home, no matter how far.

Now, as I journey through life's winding road,
I carry your teachings, your love bestowed.
Your spirit, a compass, forever will be,
In every act of kindness, a piece of you in me.

Thank you, Paa, for every word you shared,
For the lessons of goodness, for the way you cared.
In my heart, your wisdom will always reside—
The preacher, my father, my eternal guide.

MY GUIDING LIGHT

Paa, you've been there, strong and true,
Through every choice, I turned to you.
With steady wisdom, you'd lend an ear,
Guiding me through each doubt and fear.

You opened doors I couldn't see,
Pushed me forward, helped me be free.
When I felt lost, your voice was near—
A compass steady, a light sincere.

From little choices to the vast unknown,
Your love and support have always shown.
You taught me to weigh what's right and wrong,
And helped me find the place I belong.

Now I'm learning to walk on my own,
But your words are etched like stone.
Thank you, Paa, for every word;
Your love echoes loudly in this world I've heard.

THE ESSENCE OF LOVE

Love is the warmth of your steady gaze,
The hand that held mine through life's maze.
It's in your laughter on simpler days,
And gentle words that paved my ways.

Love is the patience you showed in doubt,
A quiet strength when the world grew loud.
It's every lesson you shared with pride,
A bond that grew as we walked side by side.

Love is the guidance you gave so true,
A promise kept, a heart that knew.
In memories woven, strong and whole,
You are the light that fills my soul.

Through every moment, in all I pursue,
Your love is here, in all that I do.
Gone from sight, yet close as breath,
You are my strength in life and death.

GUIDED BY YOUR CALM

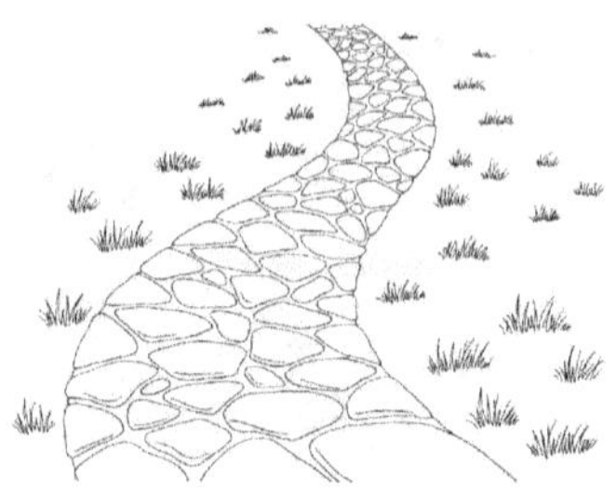

Paa, your patience was a boundless sea,
A calm embrace that sheltered me.
In moments when the world rushed by,
You stood unwavering, a gentle sky.

With every challenge, you took your time,
Teaching resilience, a virtue sublime.
Through storms of doubt and waves of fear,
Your quiet strength was always near.

You listened deeply, never rushed;
In your presence, all worries hushed.
I strive to mirror your patient ways,
Yet feel the distance of those days.

For in your calm, I've learned to see,
A love that's enduring, wild and free.
Though I may falter and sometimes stray,
Your legacy guides me, come what may.

A FLAME IN MY HEART

I miss the bonfire, the crackling glow,
The warmth of the flames in the evening's flow.
With roasted potatoes, golden and sweet,
We gathered around, where laughter would meet.

The steam from our tea curled up in the air,
A comforting hug in the cool evening flare.
We'd sip and we'd savour, with stories to share,
Each moment a treasure, beyond all compare.

Through travels we ventured, exploring the lands,
With you by my side, my heart in your hands.
The talks we would have, deep into the night,
Every word woven into a tapestry bright.

From mountains to valleys, we wandered with glee,
In the simplest moments, you and me.
The warmth of your spirit, the love that you gave,
In those cherished memories, I'll forever save.

So, here's to the fires, the laughter, the tea,
The journeys we took, just you and me.
Though time moves on and days may depart,
In my soul, you live on, a flame in my heart.

FLAVOURFUL MEMORIES

I miss the barbecues, the sizzle and smoke,
The laughter we shared, the stories we spoke.
With grilled delights, you'd tend to the flame,
Creating deliciousness, never quite the same.

We'd come together, loved ones all near,
With laughter and stories, hearts full of cheer.
Each bite was a memory, seasoned with love,
A taste of togetherness, blessings from above.

And how we'd indulge in ice cream so sweet,
Scoops of pure joy, a summer's retreat.
With sprinkles and smiles, we'd savour each bite,
In those simple pleasures, everything felt right.

You'd whip up fresh juice, a colourful blend,
Refreshing and bright, a treat without end.
Sharing those moments, our hearts intertwined;
In every flavour, your love was defined.

Now as I sit in silence, I long for those days,
For the taste of your kindness in so many ways.
Though barbecues fade and ice cream may melt,
In my heart, those flavours of love will be felt.

A HEART OF THANKSGIVING

Paa, you showed me the way to truly see,
The beauty in gratitude, the spirit to simply be.
With every lesson, you'd gently remind,
To thank God for blessings, both big and blind.

In moments of joy and times of despair,
You taught me to find Him, always there.
Through prayer and whispers, in quiet grace,
We learned to seek Him, to find our place.

You'd say, 'In all things, give thanks and praise,
For life's little gifts in so many ways'.
With a heart full of love, you'd stand and pray,
Planting seeds of gratitude to bloom each day.

Now, I carry your words deep in my soul,
A thankful heart that makes me whole.
In every sunrise, in every sigh,
I thank God for you, my guiding sky.

THE LANGUAGE OF LOVE

Paa, your strength was gentle, your heart so wide,
A calming presence, my steady guide.
You never raised your voice or hand;
Instead, you taught me how to understand.

In a world where chaos often reigns,
You showed me peace, easing all pains.
With every word, you spoke so soft,
Lifting me up, helping me loft.

No trace of anger, just love's embrace,
In your warm gaze, I always found my place.
You taught me kindness, patience and grace–
With each tender moment, I felt your trace.

Through trials faced and storms that blew,
You led by example in all you'd do.
A quiet strength, a heart so true;
In your language of love, I learned from you.

Now, as I walk my own path each day,
I carry your lessons in every way.
Your legacy lives on, a guiding star;
In the language of love, you're never far.

PAA'S GENTLE STRENGTH

When exams approached, you knew my fears,
With quiet strength, you calmed my tears.
You'd gather goodies from the bakery's best–
Sweet little comforts to help me rest.

With every treat, your love was clear,
A thoughtful touch to ease my year.
You filled my desk with supplies galore,
Stationery stacked, and always more.

Never a whisper of pressure to succeed,
You taught me the value of a good name, indeed.
'Do your best', you'd say, 'let your heart lead,
In kindness and honour, plant every seed'.

You showed me that grades weren't all that count,
But the person I am, the love I amount.
In those moments, your care was my light,
Guiding me softly through every long night.

Now, as I face the trials ahead,
I carry your lessons, the words you said.
In every challenge, I hear your refrain,
'Be true to yourself; that's how you'll gain'.

SHOPPING ADVENTURES

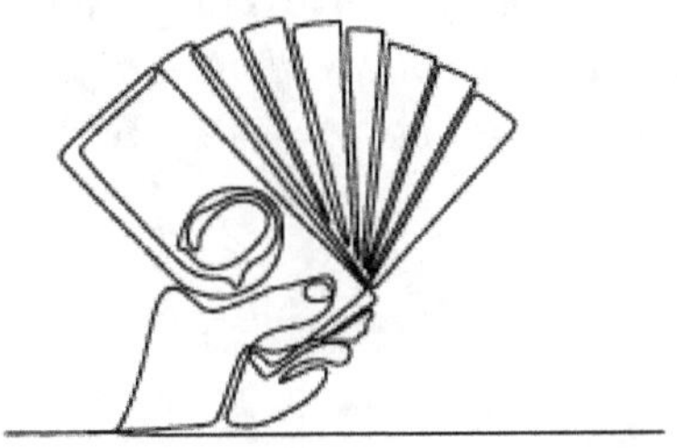

I remember those days, walking down each aisle,
Your smile so warm, your gaze so mild.
'Pick what you like', you'd always say,
No questions asked, in your easy way.

I'd hold up things, look at the price,
But you'd shake your head, so calm, so nice.
'It's beautiful, let's get it – it's yours', you'd say,
A little gift to brighten my day.

Silver and crystal, delicate and fine,
You gathered these treasures, said they were mine.
Each piece a memory, sparkling and clear,
A part of you I hold so dear.

Now when I shop, it's never the same,
Without you there to lift each frame.
No one to say, 'It's a gift; just take it',
Or to make me smile when I hesitate.

I wear these jewels; they glow like you,
Each one a reminder, timeless and true.
Though I search the aisles alone today,
Your love surrounds me in every way.

SWEET REMINDERS OF LOVE

When I chose to bunk college, a mischievous
spark,
I'd turn to you, Paa, my safe harbour, my ark.
With a knowing smile, you'd listen with care,
Understanding my heart, our bond so rare.

'Just a day off', I'd say with a grin,
You'd nod and chuckle, gently letting me in.
In those moments, we shared laughter and light,
A secret connection that felt just right.

You never judged; you just opened your heart,
Embracing my choices, a true work of art.
I'm grateful now for the memories we made,
The warmth of your love will never fade.

Thank you, Paa, for those carefree days,
For your quiet support, your gentle ways.
Though you're gone, your memories stay near,
In each cherished memory, I hold you here.

In every decision, your thoughts I'll find,
A love so profound, forever entwined.
With gratitude, I walk on, your laughter in mind,
For the gift of those moments, so rare and kind.

INSPIRING STYLE AND WISDOM

*In college halls, where the young souls would
roam,*
*There walked a professor who made every place
home.*
The best-dressed Paa, with a style so refined,
In suits and flair, you left the ordinary behind.

Sharp-minded and bright, you taught with ease,
The smartest around, setting minds at peace.
With polished shoes and a smile so keen,
You were elegance defined, a sight to be seen.

Not a wrinkle dared to mar your face,
Perfect and poised, a man of grace.
Even models would nod, 'Who's this man we see?
Outshining us all, as fine as can be'!

In every place, you'd command the air,
With a spark of brilliance beyond compare.
The brightest, the kindest, so perfect and true—
In my heart, dear Paa, there's no one like you.

A MODEL OF GRACE

Paa, you're a model, a ray of light,
A preacher of love, guiding with insight.
With a heart full of kindness and faith so deep,
You taught me to nurture the promises we keep.

Your generosity flowed like a river so wide,
In giving and caring, you took such pride.
You showed me the beauty in helping others,
A legacy woven in love for each other.

Your love for God was a radiant flame,
In every prayer, you honoured His name.
With dedication to the church, you stood tall,
Like a guiding light, embracing us all.

And in taking care of yourself, you would say,
'Body and spirit must thrive every day'.
You taught me that balance is key to our flight,
To honour this life with grace and might.

So, here's to you, Paa, my model, my guide,
With lessons of faith and love as my stride.
In every moment, your wisdom I see—
A reflection of grace, forever in me.

THE JOY YOU BROUGHT

*In a world filled with laughter, you were the
brightest light,
Your humour, like sunshine, made everything right.
With every joke you told and every smile you
shared,
You brought joy to our lives, showing how deeply
you cared.*

*The way you would chuckle, that twinkle in your
eye,
You turned mundane moments into reasons to fly.
Through laughter and stories, you wove a strong
bond,
With every little quip, you forged a love beyond.*

Now in the silence, your absence feels near,
I miss the sound of your laughter, warmth of your
cheer.
Though life feels heavy, I still carry your spark,
For in every shared memory, you light up the dark.

So, here's to you, Paa, the master of glee,
Your spirit lives on in every smile I see.
Though I ache for your laughter, your voice in the
air,
I'll honour your joy, for you taught me to care.

In my heart, you remain, a treasure so true,
For the gift of your laughter is a love that renews.
Though I miss you deeply, I'll keep your joy alive,
For in making others smile, your legacy will
thrive.

CHERISHED MEMORIES

Paa, there's a void that nothing can fill,
In the quiet moments, I feel you still.
Your laughter echoes in my heart's embrace,
Each memory cherished, time can't erase.

I miss your subjects, the lessons you'd share,
The way you taught with kindness and care.
Your voice would resonate, soothing and warm,
Guiding me gently through every storm.

'Monu ma', you'd call, with a smile so bright;
'Mona', you'd say, turning darkness to light.
'Magalae', your words wrapped around me tight,
A melody of love, my heart's pure delight.

In every syllable, your affection was clear,
A language of love that I forever hold so dear.
Now, as I walk this path on my own,
I carry your essence; in my heart, you've grown.

Though you may be gone, your presence remains,
In the way I live, in my joys and my pains.
So here's to you, Paa, in all that I do,
I'll cherish your memory, forever true.

THE HEART OF GENEROSITY

In a world where kindness often goes unseen,
You shone like a star, a heart evergreen.
Paa, your generosity knew no bounds;
In every gesture, pure love abounds.

With open hands, you gave without measure,
Sharing your blessings, your greatest treasure.
From helping a neighbour to lending a hand,
Your spirit of giving, a beautiful strand.

You taught me that wealth is not just in gold,
But in love and compassion, we choose to uphold.
Every smile you shared, every moment you spent,
Reflected the beauty of your heart's intent.

You'd listen to stories of those in need,
And act without hesitation, planting each seed.
With a warmth that embraced, you inspired us all;
In the face of hardship, you'd answer the call.

Now, as I walk this journey on my own,
Your lessons of generosity have brightly shone.
In each act of kindness, in every warm deed,
I carry your memory; it's love that I seed.

So, here's to you, Paa, a model so true,
A testament to giving in all that you do.
Your legacy of love will forever endure,
In the hearts of those you touched, kind and pure.

ECHOES OF YOUR CHEER

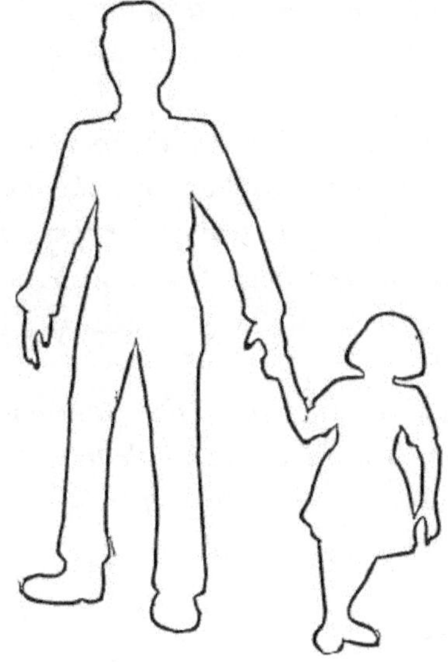

In every candle lit, on every birthday cake,
In every wish made, for life's dreams to awake,
You were there, with laughter, so steady and true,
The joy in each moment – made brighter by you.

For every small triumph, you stood by my side,
Eyes filled with pride, my strength, my guide.
When I held up my trophies, you'd cheer loud and
clear,
Now silence remains, where once was your cheer.

We celebrated big days – first home, bike and car,
Each one a milestone, each one a star.
But now as I stand, with awards in my hand,
It's only your absence I can barely withstand.

Though tears fill my eyes and the room feels cold,
The memories of you are treasures of gold.
For every achievement, I know in my heart,
You're there in the echoes, though we're worlds
apart.

So, I carry your pride, like a flame burning bright,
Guiding me forward, a soft, gentle light.
And though you're not here, your love will remain,
Forever my joy, my strength and my gain.

A LEGACY OF ENCOURAGEMENT

With every word you spoke, a spark ignited inside,
You taught me the value of hard work and pride.
'Be sincere in your efforts', you'd gently remind,
'Trust that God has a plan and the right path you'll
find'.

Through long days and late nights, your faith
never wavered,
In the struggles I faced, your wisdom was
favoured.
You showed me that effort is the key to succeed,
And in the depths of my heart, I knew I'd be freed.

You cheered for my triumphs; you soothed every
fear,
With love as my anchor, you made everything clear.
'Keep striving for greatness; don't ever lose sight,
In diligence and kindness, you'll always find light'.

*Though the road may be rocky and storms may
arise,
I carry your lessons; they lift me to the skies.
For every challenge I meet, I'll remember your
grace,
And in becoming your daughter, I'll honour your
place.*

IN THE GARDEN OF MEMORY

In the garden where you lingered, where orchids bloomed with grace,
You found a world of wonder in every fragrant space.
With hands so gentle, nurturing each petal and leaf,
You shared your love of flowers, a bond beyond belief.

As I sat there feeling restless, watching time drift slowly by,
I didn't grasp the beauty then, beneath the open sky.
Now, I tend these orchids, with memories held so dear,
Each blossom tells a story, whispers that you're still here.

With every vibrant colour, I see your spirit shine,
In the soft and tender petals, your love feels divine.
You taught me how to cherish the beauty all
around,
In every bloom that opens, your presence can be
found.

Though time has taken you away and silence fills
the space,
Your passion lives within me, in every flower's
grace.
So as I water and nurture, I carry you along—
In the garden of my heart, you're forever where I
belong.

EMBRACING THE FLAME

In the crucible of life, I've melted and been forged,
From the ashes of sorrow, a stronger self emerged.
Facing every challenge, I've found my true voice,
In the depths of despair, I learned how to rejoice.

Though you've left this world, your spirit remains,
You taught me lessons through joys and pains.
Your teachings, like embers, still flicker and glow,
Illuminating my path, helping me grow.

Trials shaped me, and I've gathered my grace,
With each step I take, I honour your space.
In sorrow, I've discovered a strength I can claim,
For the fire of loss has kindled my flame.

So, here's to the warmth of the love that we shared,
A bond that transcends, a connection declared.
In the journey of life, I embrace every part,
For in becoming your daughter, I'm learning my heart.

A CANVAS OF INDEPENDENCE

Each day unfolds like a canvas white,
With brushstrokes of courage, painted in light.
You were the artist, guiding my hand;
Now I paint my own, learning to stand.

In the absence of your wise embrace,
I've carved my path and found my place.
Missing you dearly, Paa, yet standing strong,
With lessons in my heart, I climb every hill along.

I won't waste a heartbeat on fleeting things,
Or emotions that tangle, like untethered strings.
The echoes of your voice remind me to rise,
To cherish the moments that truly define.

Every challenge I meet with a fearless grin,
For I know that you're watching, guiding within.
Your words ignite the flame of my fight;
I walk on, carrying your love, my eternal light.

REFLECTIONS OF GROWTH

In mirrors that show my ever-evolving face,
I see the strength, born of your grace.
No longer adrift in seas of despair,
With every wave, I learn to declare.

You taught me the value of time well spent,
How to be fierce and when to relent,
In the wake of your passing, I've found my way;
No more idle moments – I seize the day.

With every misstep, I stand a bit tall;
Your absence is loud, yet I feel your call.
To push through the doubt, to let go of the fear,
For life's too short and precious to linger here.

I weave my own story, thread by thread,
A beautiful life, where dreams are fed,
You are the wind beneath my wings;
In the silence, your legacy sings.

STRENGTH IN YOUR TEACHINGS

In every word you spoke, I found a guiding star,
Taught me to stand tall, no matter where we are.
With laughter as my armour, love my gentle shield,
I carry on with courage, in every wound healed.

Though shadows may surround me, I'll find the
light within,
Your lessons are whispers that ignite my will to
win.
Facing every challenge, I'll wear your smile with
pride,
You taught me to rise again, with strength deep
inside.

So, here's to the strength you gifted from above,
In the journey ahead, I'll walk with your love.
Each step I take, I feel you close and near;
Your spirit lives in me, dispelling every fear.

THE DEFINITION OF LOVE

In every hug you gave, I felt a warmth so rare;
In laughter and silence, love was always there.
Taught me what it means to care without
condition;
In your eyes, I found a world, love beyond
definition.

With every gentle lesson, you crafted who I am;
Your kindness, like sunrise, lit hope's gentle flame.
Through trials and triumphs, your support was my
guide;
On the journey of my life, you stood always by my
side.

You showed me how to love with an open heart and
mind,
To cherish every moment, to be thoughtful and
kind.

In your embrace, I found a safe and sacred space,
You are my heart's compass, my forever resting
place.

So, here's to you, dear Paa, my hero and my friend,
The embodiment of love that will never see an end.
In every beat of my heart, in every dream I weave,
I carry your love, and in you, I believe.

A TESTAMENT OF LOVE

In the quiet of the night, your whispers still remain,
A web of memories woven through my pain.
*Though you've left this world, your memories
linger near,*
In every challenge I face, I feel you guiding here.

You taught me the value of standing up tall,
To rise through the struggle, to never fear the fall.
*With every word you spoke, a seed of strength you
sowed,*
*In the garden of my heart, your love continues to
grow.*

When I stumble and falter, I recall your grace,
Your laughter, your wisdom, your warm embrace.
Though life feels heavy and the road seems long,
I carry your lessons; in your love, I am strong.

You showed me the beauty in working with pride,
To face new challenges with courage as my guide.
So here's to you, dear Dad, my hero from above,
Your legacy of strength is a testament to love.

In every step I take, I honour your name,
For in the journey ahead, my heart will remain the
same.
You are the light within me, the fire in my fight,
From you, I draw strength, my everlasting light.

THE GIFT OF CLARITY

In the haze of heartache, a new clarity blooms,
A garden of lessons where courage resumes.
You were my compass, my anchor, my guide;
Now I walk boldly, with you by my side.

Every misstep becomes a lesson to learn,
A flame rekindled with each twist and turn.
I refuse to waste time on what drags me down,
For your love is my armour, my invisible crown.

I cherish each heartbeat, each breath that I take;
In the wake of your loss, I've learned what's at
stake.
No longer a prisoner to fear or regret,
I dance in the rain, with no room for fret.

With eyes wide open, I savour the days,
Finding joy in the little things in myriad ways.
You taught me resilience; you showed me the fight,
In the depths of my sorrow, I find my own light.

A NEW HORIZON

In the twilight of memory, I search for the sun,
Each day is a journey; another battle is won.
You taught me to face the storms as they come,
To find strength in silence, to hum my own drum.

Your love was my anchor, your laughter my guide,
Now I carry it forward, with each wide stride.
No time for the trivial, the worries, the fear,
I embrace the richness, the moments held near.

With every misstep, I find my own way,
Embracing the lessons that come with each day.
For in the heart of struggles, I blossom and grow,
Your memories within me, a fire in the flow.

I rise from the shadows, my inside reclaimed,
Discovering strength in the love that remains.
You are the strength in the wind at my back,
With every heartbeat, I'm on the right track.

TURNING GRIEF INTO GROWTH

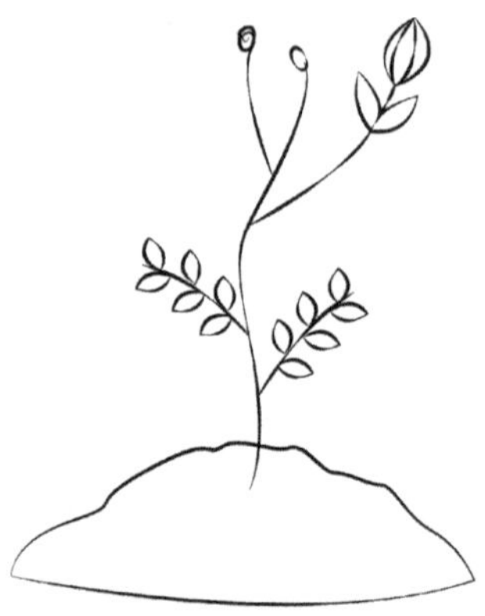

In the dawn of a new day's light,
I find my heart has taken flight.
No longer bound by the chains of grief,
I stand renewed with lots of relief.

No longer haunted by the night,
Your memory shines ever bright.
In the warmth of healing's tender glow,
A garden where new hopes grow.

With every heartbeat, strong and free,
I honour all you've given me.
Completely healed, I rise above,
A testament to your endless love.

The journey long, the path once steep,
Now I walk with roots that run deep.
In the light of a new dawn's golden gleam,
I craft and live my life; I chase my dream.

Healed and whole, I embrace each day
With your love guiding me along my way.
In the echoes of your cherished song,
I've found my place, where I belong.

EMERGING IN STRENGTH

Through sorrow that twists and rends my heart,
In pain and tears, I have found my part.
To live a life that honours you
In every step and choice, in all I pursue.

Your strength now courses through my veins,
Turning my tears into healing rains.
Amid the heartache, I rise and discover
The power to stand, to heal, to recover.

From ashes of despair, I begin to bloom;
Your presence lingers, dispelling the gloom.
In the quiet moments, I hear your voice,
A melody guiding me, making me rejoice.

For in the love you have left behind,
I find true strength, eternal and kind.
A daughter reborn, strong and true,
Forever carrying the very best of you.

DISCOVERING INNER STRENGTH

In the garden where you used to bloom,
Shadows remain, casting silent gloom.
Though sorrow whispers and looms,
I find my strength in dispelling all doom.

Yet, your wisdom lingers in the air,
A gentle presence, beyond compare.
Your presence wraps around me, a quiet embrace,
A steady glow in life's shadowed space.

At every sunrise, I resume
The journey of strength found through you.
In every heartache, I rise and bloom
A rising daughter finding her rightful room.

Every flower reminds me of you and your grace,
A beauty that never fades or erase.
With every smile, I warmly embrace
Life with all its vibrant shades.

FINDING LIGHT IN DARKNESS

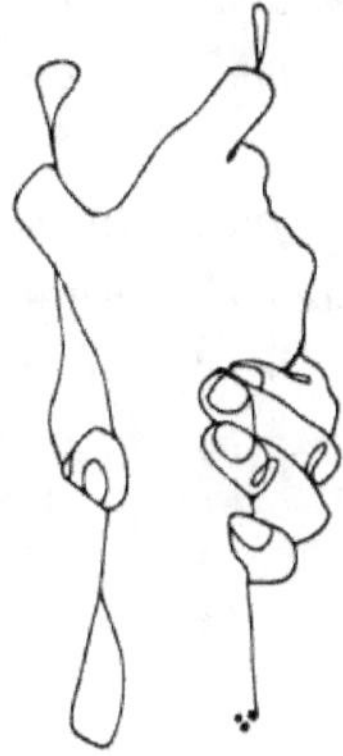

I've mended my wounds and been reborn;
In my heart, a part will always be torn.
Though grief always lingers, its shadow vast,
Yet, healing warmth has finally come to last.

I have made way for peace to reside,
For gentle ease, where hope and love collide.
In this light, where dreams and strength abide,
I find my heart's compass, a true guide.

I've learned to cherish you and be bold;
Through the pain, a strength unfolds.
At every step, I feel vibrantly renewed,
A life recharged with gratitude imbued.

With every dawn, a new chance is born;
In the light of healing, my spirit adorn.
Into a place of calm and tender grace,
Joy and love have found their place.

Fully healed, I now spread my wings,
In the motivation each day brings.
Grateful for the lessons I've learned,
In light's embrace, my heart has yearned.

ECHOES OF PAA

In quiet moments, I feel you near,
A presence so strong, a voice so clear.
We share a bond so deep and true;
In every heartbeat, I feel you.

I think of holding your steady hands—
How together we walked, you helped me stand.
Our connection, Paa, will never fade;
Your presence surrounds me, a comforting shade.

A comfort beyond spoken words,
I still hear your voice, like the songs of birds.
Reminds me of our choice, so similar and good,
Expressing your love as only you could.

Though I grieve and miss you so,
In your strength, I've begun to grow.
With every step, I honour you,
Blooming strong as you'd want me to.

RISING FROM THE ASHES

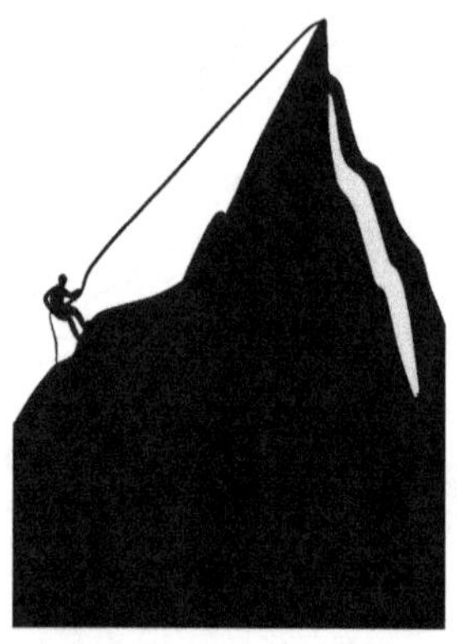

Being alone is a fear, Paa;
Like you, I can trust no one so far.
So I am becoming wiser, Paa;
I think before I reach the shore.

I invest my time, emotions and more
In things that matter and truly endure.
I can't seem to close the door;
I can't afford to roar and pour.

I see a path unfolding ahead;
I am moving on, no longer misled.
With you in my heart, I'm never cold,
Your love keeps me warm, steady and bold.

With every step, your presence is near
A guiding hand, a voice so sincere.
In your absence, I rebuild and restore
The wisdom you planted in my heart's core.

UNSEEN PRESENCE

You are my guiding star, Paa;
Your voice whispers in my mind.
You are my comfort zone, Paa;
I feel your presence by my side.

In memories, your voice rings very clear;
Your lessons guide me year by year.
In every challenge, every trial,
You have filled my heart with a smile.

In your absence, Paa, I found my might;
Though unseen, you will never be out of sight.
The seed you planted deep within
Has grown to trees, though times were grim.

Though I walk alone, I find you within—
My strength, my compass, my guide.
In my heart, your love will forever shine,
A presence eternal, both steady and sublime.

STRENGTH IN SORROW

Through the sorrow, through the pain,
I've found a strength I can't explain.
In your absence, I start to see,
The quiet fire you passed to me.

I walk alone, yet feel you near,
With every step, you ease my fear.
Though you're not here, I've come to know,
In your loving embrace, I'll always grow.

When life feels heavy, the skies turn grey,
I hear your voice that lights my way.
A whisper soft, a steady hand,
Guiding me to truly understand.

You taught me strength I didn't know,
That in this life, we learn and grow.
To stand up tall, to face my fears,
To carry on despite all the tears.

Though time may pass and years may fade,
Our bond remains, unbroken, unfrayed.
My guiding light, my constant star,
Forever near, though seeming far.

WITH YOU IN MY HEART

In the stillness of night, when shadows creep,
I feel your presence, a comfort to keep.
Though time has moved on and you're far away,
Your love is a light that remains on my way.

With every sunrise, I see your smile,
A memory woven through each passing mile.
In laughter and tears, you're never apart,
For I carry you with me, deep in my heart.

Your wisdom echoes in the choices I make,
Each lesson you taught me, a road I now take.
I treasure the moments, the laughter, the care,
In the fabric of love, your presence is always there.

Though sorrow may linger and shadows may fall,
I stand tall in your love; I stand through it all.
For you are the strength that fuels my fight,
A ray of hope in the darkest of nights.

With you in my heart, I rise and I strive,
In the dance of this life, I will always survive.
So I'll honour your legacy, my dear guiding star,
For with you in my heart, I will always go far.

A HEARTFELT THANK YOU

Thank you, dear Paa, for the memories so bright,
For the laughter of childhood, pure joy in the light.
You filled my days with stories and dreams,
In your warm embrace, life burst at the seams.

You were my professor, with wisdom to share,
Guiding me gently, showing how much you care.
In the halls of my college, your lessons rang true,
With each step I took, I carried pieces of you.

A friend in my laughter, my confidant in tears,
You listened and comforted me, calming my fears.
Your words were a lamp, a light in the dark,
You showed me the way, igniting my spark.

As my pillar of strength, you stood by my side,
In the journey of life, you were my infallible guide.
Though now you are gone, your love still remains,
In the beautiful memories, I cherish the gains.

So, here's my heartfelt thanks for all that you gave,
For the love you showered, for the path you paved.
In every cherished moment, I'll carry you near,
For you live in my heart, forever held dear.

IN GRATITUDE TO YOU, PAA

Thank you, dear Paa, for the path that you laid,
For showing me the way, where love's light,
stayed.
You taught me to seek what leads to God's feet,
In the warmth of your words, my life's sweet.

You showed me that riches fade fast like the night,
But a good name shines bright, a beacon of light.
With kindness and grace, you taught me to give,
In the heart of selfless generosity, we truly live.

*You whispered of strength that comes from the
meek,
That true power lies beyond words that we speak.
With humility's armour, we always rise above,
In the beauty of compassion, I found endless love.*

*So, here's my heartfelt gratitude, deep from my
core,
For guiding my steps, for just so much more.
In every lesson learned, your love I embrace,
Thank you, dear Paa, for your infinite grace.*

AT THE FEET OF GOD

Dear Paa, you taught me to kneel and pray,
To stay at the feet of God, come what may.
With a heart full of love, you showed me the light,
To be humble and good, to hold my dreams tight.

You urged me to thank the guardian angels above,
For their watchful protection, their infinite love.
In every whispered prayer, I feel your embrace,
A reminder of faith, of hope and of grace.

With each gentle word, you nurtured my soul;
In the melody of life, you made me feel whole.
We sang, 'God Will Make a Way', side by side,
Believing in promise, with faith as our guide.

*So, thank you, dear Paa, for the love that won't
cease,
For the strength you've instilled, for the moments
of peace.
With gratitude overflowing, I lift up my voice,
In the presence of blessings, I'll forever rejoice.*

*Here at God's feet, I offer my praise,
For the gift of your love, in so many ways.
With each whispered prayer, I feel your embrace,
Guiding me gently through life's winding race.*

A LIFE OF BLESSING

In every moment shared, your life was a gift,
A fountain of love, you always uplift.
With laughter and kindness, touching every heart,
In the journey of life, you played the finest part.

Your wisdom was timeless, your spirit so bright,
You showed me the way, like stars in the night.
A life of blessings, in all that you gave,
You spread joy and warmth, a heart brave.

In the garden of memories, your love will remain,
Through laughter and tears, through joy and pain.
You taught me to cherish the simple and the small,
In the legacy of love, you've inspired us all.

So, here's to your journey, a life deeply lived,
A testament of grace in all that you've did.
Though you may be gone, your light still shines on,
In the hearts that you've touched, your spirit lives on.

SWEET PAIN, STRONG HOPE

In the stillness of night, when stars brightly shine,
I dream of a reunion where your heart meets mine.
A hope of our meeting that fills my heart's space,
The promise of finding you in that heavenly place.

Where laughter will echo and sorrows will cease,
In the light of forever, my soul will find peace.
Where joy surrounds us and fear will take flight,
Together we'll bask in love's endless light.

With each whispered prayer, I feel you draw near,
Your love, like a shield, dispels my fear.
In that radiant moment, our hearts will intertwine,
A bond that can't be broken, a love so divine.

So, I wait with a heart full of dreams yet untold,
For the day we unite, where love will unfold.
Until then, dear Paa, I hold you so tight,
In my heart, you'll forever be my guiding light.

A GIFT FROM ABOVE

Dear God,
Thank you for blessing me with a Paa so strong,
A gift you have given, even before I asked for long.
In his gentle embrace, I found shelter and peace,
Through his love, my worries began to cease.

He's a beacon of wisdom, guiding me each day,
The strength in his laughter chased fears away.
In moments of doubt, his faith lit my way,
A testament that love is life's greatest display.

I'm grateful, Oh God, for this bond that we share,
For the lessons he taught, for his endless care.
This blessing is boundless, like the stars up above,
A testament to your grace, a father's pure love.

With every memory cherished, I hold him so near,
In the heart of my journey, he'll always be here.
Thank you, dear God, for this life's sweetest part,
For the love of my dad, forever in my heart.

THANK YOU, GOD, FOR MY PAA

Thank you, God, for the gift of my Paa,
Who led me to you with a heart full of awe.
With faith as our compass, he showed me the way;
In every prayer whispered, he brightened my day.

He taught me that God is the heart of it all;
In joy and in sorrow, I could always call.
With love in his words and grace in his hand,
He steadied my spirit, helping me stand.

Through trials and triumphs, he shared your light,
Instilling in me a faith burning so bright.
With every embrace, he nurtured my soul,
Showing me, dear God, how to feel whole.

*In his laughter and lessons, your presence shines
through,
For my dad was your servant, steadfast and true.
Thank you, dear God, for this love I can see,
For the way that he led and taught me to be.*

*So here in my heart, I'll carry him near,
With gratitude eternal, I hold him so dear.
Thank you, God, for my dad, my guide,
For the faith that he nurtured, forever my pride.*

www.ingramcontent.com/pod-product-compliance
Lightning Source LLC
Chambersburg PA
CBHW071328140726
47996CB00005B/1868